MENTAL HEALTH SUPPORT

LIVING WITH BIPOLAR DISORDER

by Tammy Gagne

BrightPoint Press

San Diego, CA

© 2024 BrightPoint Press
an imprint of ReferencePoint Press, Inc.
Printed in the United States

For more information, contact:
BrightPoint Press
PO Box 27779
San Diego, CA 92198
www.BrightPointPress.com

ALL RIGHTS RESERVED.

No part of this work covered by the copyright hereon may be reproduced or used in any form or by any means—graphic, electronic, or mechanical, including photocopying, recording, taping, web distribution, or information storage retrieval systems—without the written permission of the publisher.

Content Consultant: Colleen A. Brenner, PhD, Associate Professor of Psychology, Loma Linda University

---

LIBRARY OF CONGRESS CATALOGING-IN-PUBLICATION DATA

Names: Gagne, Tammy, author.
Title: Living with bipolar disorder / by Tammy Gagne.
Description: San Diego, CA: BrightPoint Press, [2024] | Series: Mental health support | Includes bibliographical references and index. | Audience: Ages 13 | Audience: Grades 7-9
Identifiers: LCCN 2023009813 (print) | LCCN 2023009814 (eBook) | ISBN 9781678206642 (hardcover) | ISBN 9781678206659 (eBook)
Subjects: LCSH: Bipolar disorder--Juvenile literature. | Bipolar disorder--Treatment--Juvenile literature.
Classification: LCC RC516 .G34 2024 (print) | LCC RC516 (eBook) | DDC 616.89/5--dc23/eng/20230414
LC record available at https://lccn.loc.gov/2023009813
LC eBook record available at https://lccn.loc.gov/2023009814

CONTENTS

CONTENT WARNING: THIS BOOK DESCRIBES SUICIDE AND SUICIDAL THOUGHTS, WHICH MAY BE TRIGGERING TO SOME READERS.

AT A GLANCE 4

INTRODUCTION 6
DEALING WITH BIPOLAR DISORDER

CHAPTER ONE 12
WHAT IS BIPOLAR DISORDER?

CHAPTER TWO 26
MEDICATION TREATMENTS

CHAPTER THREE 36
THERAPY TREATMENTS

CHAPTER FOUR 48
STIGMA AND SUPPORT

Glossary 58
Source Notes 59
For Further Research 60
Index 62
Image Credits 63
About the Author 64

AT A GLANCE

- Bipolar disorder is a mental illness. It involves severe mood swings. People with this disorder experience periods of extreme highs. They also have devastating lows.

- A person's chance of getting bipolar disorder increases if a biological parent has it. The risk is even higher if both parents have it.

- Most people with bipolar disorder treat the condition with medication. Finding the right combination of medications can take time.

- Therapy teaches people how to manage their bipolar disorder. There are several types of therapies from which a patient and doctor may choose.

- Family members who have a loved one with bipolar disorder may benefit from going to family therapy. A patient with a good support system has a greater chance of managing the illness well.

- People with bipolar disorder may worry that others judge them for their illness. But people should not be defined by their disorder.

- Bipolar disorder can be challenging. But people can successfully manage it. Many people with this illness lead happy and fulfilling lives.

INTRODUCTION

DEALING WITH BIPOLAR DISORDER

Loud music woke Sarah. It was the middle of the night. The music came from her brother's bedroom. She wondered if Martin was having a **manic** episode. He had bipolar disorder. This is a mental illness. It sometimes made Martin depressed. At other times, he had a lot of energy. Martin did not mean to annoy anyone with his music. He could not always control himself when mania struck. Still, his illness could be hard on the family.

It can be hard to live with someone who has bipolar disorder. But a family can work together to manage it.

Sarah's mom knocked lightly on her door. Then she opened it. "Martin is having a rough night," she said. "Dad and I will try to get him back to bed."

Sarah nodded. Sometimes she wished that she didn't have to deal with her brother's mental illness. The family therapist told her it was OK to feel that way.

Sarah knew Martin didn't like having his illness either. He had to come home from college because of it. He planned to go back to school. But he had to get his illness under control first. His doctor put him on medication. It was supposed to help

A sibling can be a good support person.

balance his moods. But it needed time to work. Martin was also seeing a therapist. For now, he needed to live at home. He had a good support system there.

TREATING BIPOLAR DISORDER

People with bipolar disorder have extreme mood swings. They may have mania and depression. During mania, people have a lot of energy. At other times, they are depressed. Each episode is different. Sometimes it lasts for hours. Other times it lasts for months. Some people have more manic episodes. Others feel depressed more often.

Mental health professionals can treat bipolar disorder. They do this in different ways. Medication helps balance the patient's mood. Which drug is best for a person depends on many things. It usually takes a few tries to find the right one. Therapy can also be helpful. It teaches

With therapy and medication, people with bipolar disorder can live happy and healthy lives.

people how to deal with the illness. It can be good for family members to see a therapist with the patient too. This can help everyone learn how to deal with the disorder better.

1

WHAT IS BIPOLAR DISORDER?

Bipolar disorder is a mental illness. People have extreme downs and ups. This affects their energy and mood. **Symptoms** of bipolar disorder include manic, hypomanic, and depressive episodes. During manic episodes, people have a lot of mental and physical energy.

Sleeping and focusing are hard. People may be excited or happy about many things all at once. Other times, people with bipolar disorder are depressed. They may not want

During a manic episode, a person might feel as if she's full of new ideas. She may not want to sleep and might talk very fast.

People who are depressed might avoid people.

to do things they normally like. They may feel hopeless about the future.

No one knows the exact causes of this illness. But research has shown that some people are more likely to get it. This includes people who have been hurt during childhood. Stressful life events may also increase a person's chances of getting the illness. This may include being bullied or losing a loved one. Some people with bipolar disorder get the illness because of their brain chemistry. Family history can also play a part.

MOST AT RISK FOR BIPOLAR DISORDER

About 2.5 percent of people in the United States have bipolar disorder. People who have a biological parent with the illness have a 10 percent chance of getting it too. Having two biological parents with the illness raises the risk to 40 percent.

Mood swings can make people feel exhausted.

There are three types of bipolar disorder. People with bipolar I have more intense manic periods. Sometimes they have manic and depressive episodes at the same time. People with bipolar II have hypomania. This is a less extreme high period. Depression is usually more intense for people with bipolar II. The third type is cyclothymia. People with this condition have both depressive and hypomanic symptoms. But they are not as strong as those experienced in bipolar I and bipolar II. Bipolar disorder is a lifelong illness. It can be managed but not cured.

HOW IS BIPOLAR DISORDER DIAGNOSED?

A person with bipolar symptoms should see a doctor. There is no test for bipolar disorder. But getting checked by a doctor

MANIC AND DEPRESSIVE SYMPTOMS

Manic Episode Symptoms	Depressive Episode Symptoms
Excitement	Feeling incredibly sad
Irritability	Feeling anxious
Lots of energy and getting less sleep	Issues with either falling and staying asleep or getting too much sleep
Racing ideas	Forgetfulness and issues with concentrating
Talking quickly about many different things	Difficulty making decisions
Wanting to do a lot of things all at once and feeling as though you won't get exhausted	Loss of interest in things you used to enjoy
Feeling very talented or important	Feeling worthless, hopeless, or suicidal

Manic episodes and depressive episodes have different sets of symptoms.

is important. It is usually the first step in

getting **diagnosed**. The doctor will do

a physical exam. He or she will also ask

questions. The doctor will want to know about any symptoms. Symptoms can last for weeks or even months. There may also be a long break between symptoms.

Primary care physicians cannot diagnose bipolar disorder. If they think someone has this condition, they send the patient to a mental health care provider. This could be a psychiatrist. Psychologists, social workers, and psychiatric nurses may also help. Once a diagnosis has been made, these professionals create a treatment plan together. They may have different but important ideas. The person with bipolar

Psychiatrists identify and treat mental illnesses.

disorder should be patient. Putting together a good plan often takes time.

Melanie McKinnon is a writer. She has bipolar disorder. She had a lot of questions after being diagnosed. She worried about how bipolar disorder would affect her.

But she soon learned that many people with the illness live happy and successful lives. "It's just getting your ducks in a row that's difficult at first," she wrote. "And it's hard to be patient, but small, positive steps over time will bring . . . lasting results."[1]

EFFECTS ON DAILY LIFE

Having bipolar disorder affects a person's life. Mood swings can make it hard to go to school or work. They may also cause the person to get into fights. This can lead to relationship problems with family and friends.

When people have mania, they are more likely to do risky things. They may act before thinking. For example, some people spend too much money. Others may drive dangerously. They may take on big tasks without being able to complete them.

BIPOLAR DISORDER AND AGE

A person can get bipolar disorder at any age. Most people have their first symptoms in their early twenties. Children and teens can get bipolar disorder too. But this disorder is often harder to diagnose in younger people. Doctors may think a young person with bipolar disorder has attention deficit hyperactivity disorder (ADHD) instead. The two conditions share many symptoms.

Halsey is a singer and songwriter. She has bipolar disorder. For a long time, it was hard for her to handle her mania. She said, "I considered that girl, the manic one . . . irresponsible and untrustworthy, unreliable. She spoke too loud. She had a million ideas and couldn't get any of them done."[2] Halsey got the help she needed. She accepted her condition. She began to do well. But it took medication and therapy to get to that point.

Selena Gomez is an actress and singer. She also has bipolar disorder. She was overwhelmed by the low periods that followed her mania. She said, "It would

Selena Gomez has been open about discussing her mental health struggles.

start with depression, then it would go into isolation. Then it was just me not being able to move from my bed. I didn't want anyone to talk to me."[3] Gomez said she even had suicidal thoughts. It took her a while to accept that she had bipolar disorder. But once she did, she was able to start learning how to handle it.

2

MEDICATION TREATMENTS

People with bipolar disorder need medication to treat it. Without medication, a person's symptoms will continue. Some people take just one medication. Others take a few drugs. Finding the right medicines can take time.

Many doctors start people on a mood stabilizer. This drug helps balance a person's mood. One of the most common mood stabilizers is lithium. It is good at both treating and preventing mania. But it isn't as good at helping with depression. For this

Medications affect the brain and help regulate it.

reason, a patient often needs to take another medication too.

Antidepressants are used to treat depression. Many types of antidepressants can be used for bipolar disorder. But some drugs can **trigger** mania. This makes taking the mood stabilizer especially important.

SAFE TREATMENT PLANS

People with bipolar disorder may have other illnesses. For example, patients might also suffer from ADHD, an anxiety disorder, or an eating disorder. In these cases, a doctor must make sure that all a patient's medications can be safely taken together.

Stomach pain is a side effect of some bipolar medications.

Antianxiety medication is also helpful. Some of these drugs can help calm a patient who has trouble sleeping. This is a symptom of both depression and mania. In the most severe cases, a person with bipolar disorder can go days without sleeping.

Bipolar medications should not be stopped suddenly. Doing so can cause side effects. These may include headaches, stomach problems, or more serious health issues. Even if a certain drug isn't helping, a patient should be weaned off it. This means slowly lowering the amount of the drug someone takes. It can take weeks to stop one medication before starting another. Doctors tell patients how best to do this with each medication. The exact combination of drugs can be different for

Insomnia is when people can't fall or stay asleep. People with bipolar disorder may suffer from this.

each patient. There are common symptoms for bipolar disorder. But each case is unique.

Dr. Sudhakar Selvaraj is a professor of psychiatry. He believes in good communication with patients. He thinks that is key to finding the right medications. "A patient needs to be involved in the decision-making from the beginning," he says.[4] Patients know how medications make them feel. They can talk to their doctors about it. They can help narrow down the best options.

SIDE EFFECTS

Bipolar disorder medications can have side effects. Some examples are headaches, nausea, blurred vision, and confusion. Sometimes the side effects go away once a person's body gets used to the medication. Doctors usually change medications if side effects are very bad.

Getting treatment for bipolar disorder can make people feel better about themselves.

HOW WELL DOES MEDICATION WORK?

The start of treatment may be hard. People might not feel better right away. This can be disappointing. Finding the right drug takes patience. Even the best medications need some time to work well. With the right medications, a person's symptoms usually get better in about three months.

Bebe Rexha is a singer and songwriter. She has bipolar disorder. Like many people, she was afraid of taking medication at first. She worried the drugs might change who she was. Rexha also worried they might limit her creativity. But she said that medication helped her focus. Rexha added that she was surprised by how much better she felt when the medication kicked in.

The right medication can make all the difference. People should stick to their treatment plans. They will find that bipolar

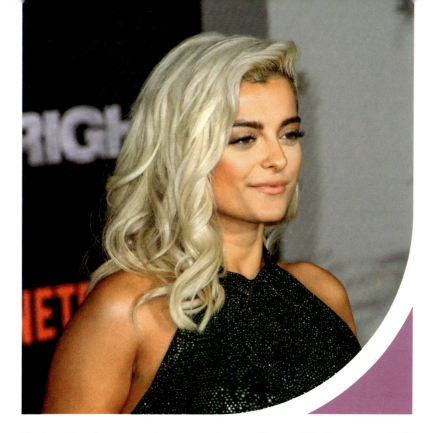

Bebe Rexha spent years struggling with her mental health before getting a bipolar disorder diagnosis.

disorder is highly treatable. According to the National Advisory Mental Health Council, the illness has a treatment success rate of 80 percent in the United States.

3

THERAPY TREATMENTS

Therapy helps many people with bipolar disorder. Talking to a mental health professional will not fully treat the illness. But therapy can be used alongside medication. This lets people successfully manage their illness.

COGNITIVE BEHAVIORAL THERAPY

Cognitive behavioral therapy (CBT) is a common treatment for bipolar disorder. In CBT, people learn how to notice their negative feelings and thoughts. They focus

Opening up may be difficult. But therapists are trained to help people navigate life's challenges.

CBT gives people the skills they need to manage strong emotions.

on being more positive. CBT teaches people that they have control over their thoughts and feelings. Therefore, they can control how they react to things.

CBT looks at symptoms of depression and mania. It addresses any negative feelings that come with the episodes, such as guilt. CBT helps people notice their moods. If a person feels an episode coming on, he or she can look for help. People also learn calming skills in CBT. They can use these skills when they feel a mood change coming. CBT can lower the number of depressive and manic episodes people have.

Patients must practice the skills they learn in CBT. That way, they will get better at them. Therapists usually give homework. People who have the most success with CBT are the ones who do all their homework.

INTERPERSONAL AND SOCIAL RHYTHM THERAPY

Another therapy used to treat bipolar disorder is interpersonal social rhythm therapy (IPSRT). It focuses on a person's daily routine. It also looks at **disruptions** that can happen. Mental health professionals call this "disruption in social rhythm." Simon Rego is a psychologist. He explains, "The term, a *disruption in*

Some people feel stressed when their routine is disrupted.

social rhythm, sounds fancy, but it really just means any change to our regular daily routines, such as the time we wake up, the times we eat our meals, and the time we go to bed."[5]

People who are struggling may take their frustration out on friends or family.

Poor sleep is one sign that a manic or hypomanic episode is coming. In IPSRT, people pay attention to their sleep habits.

They may see signs of poor sleep. If that happens, they can use skills learned in therapy to help handle an episode.

IPSRT also looks at people's relationships. It is normal to have disagreements from time to time. But for people with bipolar disorder, personal conflicts can trigger mania. IPSRT lowers the chances of this happening. It teaches people useful coping skills. Stephen Ferrando is a psychiatrist. He says, "The individual learns to manage conflict and thus avoid a manic episode that can do a lot of damage."[6]

Bipolar disorder may affect the whole family. Therapy can help people get through any struggles.

FAMILY AND GROUP THERAPY

Bipolar disorder can affect people's loved ones. Family therapy can be helpful. It gives everyone a safe place to talk about their feelings. Families can also learn more about the illness during therapy. It helps the patient and loved ones create plans for the future.

Group therapy is different from family therapy. It brings many people with bipolar disorder together. They talk about their illness. People can share both the hard

A GOOD START

Family therapy is important at the beginning stages of bipolar disorder treatment. In most cases, family members go to about twelve sessions with their loved one. Early sessions focus on learning about the illness. Later, the focus often moves to communication and problem-solving skills.

and good times in the group setting. They

can share skills that have worked for them.

They can also ask for advice. Talking about

bipolar disorder with other people who

have the illness is helpful. People may feel

understood and supported.

BEING UNDERSTOOD

Experts say the type of therapy used to treat bipolar disorder is less important than other things. For example, they think the comfort level the patient feels with the therapist or group matters much more. People with bipolar disorder benefit from being around those who understand what they are going through.

Talking to friends, family, and others who have a mental illness can help people manage their own mental health struggles.

47

4

STIGMA AND SUPPORT

There is **stigma** around mental illness. People may unfairly see someone with a mental disorder in a bad light. The stigma is often worse when it comes to bipolar disorder. Marcia Purse is a mental health writer. She said, "Individuals with bipolar are often [shown] as 'crazy' in books and movies and quite often, these individuals commit crimes or aren't able to live independently."[7] Some people do not understand bipolar disorder. They might believe what they see in books and movies.

Stigma can lead to bullying.

Then they judge people in real life who have this illness.

People with bipolar disorder may feel embarrassed or judged. They may worry that people won't want to be their friends. This makes the illness even harder to manage. Some people might not seek treatment. They may not want to be labeled as having bipolar disorder. Some people may stop taking their medications because they feel so judged.

Many people with bipolar disorder find group therapy helpful for this reason. Other people with the illness know how hard it

Feeling alone can make a mental health crisis more difficult to handle.

can be. Also, therapists can help people deal with their feelings about stigma. They can help patients find ways to cope with it.

OTHER TREATMENTS

Light therapy helps some people with bipolar disorder. These people may have bad depression in the winter. That is because it is dark outside for long periods of time. The treatment process is simple. A person turns on a special light. He or she sits in front of it for about thirty minutes each day. This has been shown to help some people's moods.

Researchers are looking at other treatments too. They hope these treatments can help people with bipolar disorder in the future. One treatment increases electrical activity in the brain. It has been used to treat depression. Some research suggests it could help treat bipolar disorder too.

Light therapy imitates sunlight. Researchers think the light triggers the brain to make chemicals that make people happier.

HELP DURING EMERGENCIES

Symptoms of bipolar disorder can get worse without treatment. In some cases, people get new symptoms, such as psychosis. That is when people see or hear things that are not there. The person cannot tell what is real and what is not. Psychosis can happen during a manic or depressive episode. Some people have to take antipsychotic medications.

A HEALTHY DIET

Eating healthy can make it easier for a person to manage bipolar disorder. Studies have shown that omega-3 fatty acids can improve brain function and mood. Experts think they may also decrease depression in people with bipolar disorder. Avoiding caffeine may also be helpful for people with this illness. Research has shown that caffeine can trigger mania. However, diet changes should not replace medication and therapy.

When people hallucinate, they're seeing or hearing things that aren't really there.

These treat symptoms of psychosis, such as **hallucinations**.

Selena Gomez experienced psychosis just before her bipolar disorder diagnosis. She was hearing voices. They kept getting louder and louder. People who cared about

Caring family and friends, along with proven treatments, can help people manage their bipolar disorder.

Gomez asked her to go to a mental health hospital. "I didn't want to," Gomez said, "but I didn't want to be trapped in myself and my mind anymore."[8] Gomez went to the hospital. She got treatment for her bipolar disorder.

Getting help can make living with bipolar disorder manageable. People with the illness face challenges. But they can live happy and healthy lives with the right treatment.

WHEN TO STEP IN

Sometimes people with bipolar disorder do not realize when treatment is needed. For example, mania makes people feel excited and hopeful. People may not think they need help for these feelings. Or they might not want to take their medication. In these situations, family members or friends can get involved. They can try to get the person help.

GLOSSARY

diagnosed
to have had a disease or illness identified

disruptions
disturbances or problems

hallucinations
experiences that involve perceiving things that are not actually present

manic
showing wild excitement or energy

stigma
a mark of disgrace or shame

symptoms
signs that an illness exists

trigger
cause to happen or exist

SOURCE NOTES

CHAPTER ONE: WHAT IS BIPOLAR DISORDER?

1. Melanie McKinnon, "Recently Diagnosed with Bipolar: 10 Ways to Start Your Journey to Stability," *bphope* (blog), August 31, 2021. www.bphope.com.

2. Quoted in "Halsey—A Conversation About Bipolar Disorder," *Los Angeles Times*, July 21, 2020. www.latimes.com.

3. Quoted in Olivia Truffaut-Wong, "Selena Gomez Opens Up About Living with Bipolar Disorder," *Cut*, November 3, 2022. www.thecut.com.

CHAPTER TWO: MEDICATION TREATMENTS

4. Quoted in "Bipolar Disorder: An Interview with Professor Sudhakar Selvaraj," *BMJ Best Practice*, May 9, 2019. https://bestpractice.bmj.com.

CHAPTER THREE: THERAPY TREATMENTS

5. Quoted in Rosemary Black, "Treatments for Bipolar Disorder: Cognitive Behavioral Therapy and More," *Psycom*, October 24, 2022. www.psycom.net.

6. Quoted in Black, "Treatments for Bipolar Disorder: Cognitive Behavioral Therapy and More."

CHAPTER FOUR: STIGMA AND SUPPORT

7. Quoted in Marcia Purse, "Living with Bipolar Disorder," *Very Well Mind*, October 17, 2021. www.verywellmind.com.

8. Quoted in Truffaut-Wong, "Selena Gomez Opens Up About Living With Bipolar Disorder."

FOR FURTHER RESEARCH

BOOKS

Kathy MacMillan, *Understanding Bipolar Disorder*. San Diego, CA: BrightPoint Press, 2021.

Richard Spilsbury, *Bipolar Disorder*. New York: Rosen, 2019.

Susan Wroble, *Living with Depression*. San Diego, CA: BrightPoint Press, 2024.

INTERNET SOURCES

"Bipolar Disorder," *TeensHealth*, August 2022. https://kidshealth.org.

Jon Johnson, "What Are the Signs of Bipolar Disorder in Teens?" *Medical News Today*, February 5, 2019. www.medicalnewstoday.com.

Cassandra Miasnikov, "Myths and Facts of Bipolar Disorder," *NAMI*, May 5, 2021. www.nami.org.

WEBSITES

American Psychological Association
www.apa.org

The American Psychological Association is a professional, scientific organization that focuses on psychology. It provides information on mental illnesses, including bipolar disorder.

Mayo Clinic
www.mayoclinic.org

The Mayo Clinic has medical centers around the country and provides information on many mental disorders, including bipolar disorder.

National Alliance on Mental Illness
www.nami.org

The National Alliance on Mental Illness advocates for people with mental illnesses so they can live happy, healthy lives.

INDEX

antianxiety, 29
antidepressants, 28
arguments, 21

bipolar I, 16–17
bipolar II, 16–17

cognitive behavioral therapy (CBT), 37–40
cyclothymia, 17

depression, 6, 10, 12–13, 16–18, 25, 27–29, 39, 52, 54
diagnose, 18–20, 22, 55
diet, 54

energy, 6, 10, 12, 18
episode, 6, 10, 12, 16, 18, 39, 42–43, 54

family therapy, 8, 44–45

Gomez, Selena, 23, 25, 55–56
group therapy, 45–46, 50

hallucinations, 55
Halsey, 23
hypomanic, 12, 17, 42

interpersonal social rhythm therapy (IPSRT), 40–43

light therapy, 51–52

manic, 6, 10, 12–13, 16, 18, 23, 39, 42–43, 54
mood stabilizer, 27–28

National Advisory Mental Health Council, 35

psychosis, 54–55

Rexha, Bebe, 34

Selvaraj, Sudhakar, 31–32
side effects, 30, 32
stigma, 48, 51
symptoms, 12, 17–19, 22, 26, 29, 31, 34, 39, 53, 55

therapist, 8–9, 11, 39, 46, 51
treatment plan, 19–20, 28, 34
trigger, 28, 43, 54

IMAGE CREDITS

Cover: © MDV Edwards/Shutterstock Images
5: © PeopleImages/iStockphoto
7: © Andrey_Popov/Shutterstock Images
9: © FG Trade/iStockphoto
11: © Phynart Studio/iStockphoto
13: © PR Image Factory/Shutterstock Images
14: © Charday Penn/iStockphoto
16: © PeopleImages/iStockphoto
18: © Red Line Editorial
20: © LightField Studios/Shutterstock Images
24: © Denis Makarenko/Shutterstock Images
27: © blackCAT/iStockphoto
29: © Dragana Gordic/Shutterstock Images
31: © PeopleImages/iStockphoto
33: © JLco/Julia Amaral/iStockphoto
35: © Carla Van Wagoner/Shutterstock Images
37: © NoSystem Images/iStockphoto
38: © SDI Productions/iStockphoto
41: © Rawpixel.com/Shutterstock Images
42: © Prostock-Studio/iStockphoto
44: © bluecinema/iStockphoto
47: © fizkes/Shutterstock Images
49: © Ground Picture/Shutterstock Images
51: © Marjan Apostolovic/Shutterstock Images
53: © Rocky89/iStockphoto
55: © Dean Mitchell/iStockphoto
56: © Pekic/iStockphoto

ABOUT THE AUTHOR

Tammy Gagne has written hundreds of books for both adults and children. Some of her recent books are about dealing with gender dysphoria and self-injury disorder. She lives in northern New England with her husband, son, and dogs.